what would you ask?
NEIL ARMSTRONG

Anita Ganeri
Illustrated by Liz Roberts

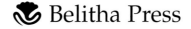 Belitha Press

First published in the UK in 1999 by
Belitha Press Limited, London House, Great Eastern
Wharf, Parkgate Road, London SW11 4NQ

ISBN 1 85561 899 0

British Library Cataloguing in Publication Data
for this book is available from the British Library.

Printed in China

10 9 8 7 6 5 4 3 2 1

Editors: Veronica Ross & Claire Edwards
Designer: Simeen Karim
Illustrator: Liz Roberts
Consultant: Hester Collicutt

Contents

What do you do?

'I am an American astronaut and pilot.'

On 20 July 1969, American astronaut Neil Armstrong
became the first person to set foot on the Moon. Watched
by millions of television viewers all over the world,
Armstrong stepped out of the lunar module and
took his first steps on the Moon's surface. 'That's
one small step for a man,' he said, 'one giant
leap for mankind.'

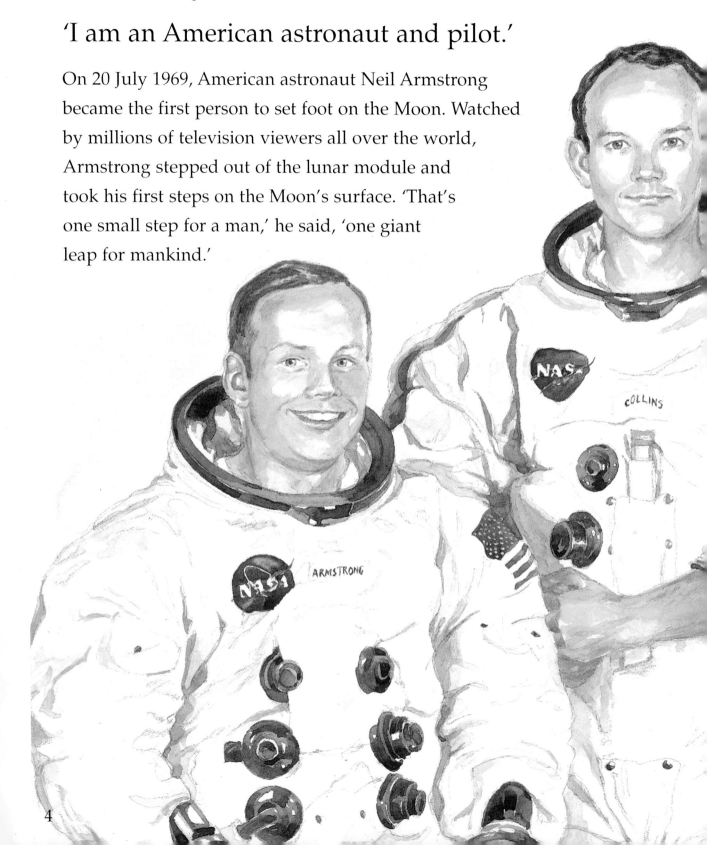

In 1957 the Russians sent the first man-made satellite, *Sputnik 1*, into space. In 1961 the Russian cosmonaut Yuri Gagarin became the first person in space. This placed the Russians ahead of their American rivals in the 'space race'. But the Americans were determined to take the lead. In May 1961 US President John F Kennedy announced that by 1970 America would put a man on the Moon.

The *Apollo 11* mission to the Moon was one of the most exciting journeys ever made. It was also one of the riskiest. No one knew exactly what the astronauts would find on the Moon, or if they would ever come back again.

Where were you born?

'I was born on my
grandparents' farm,
near Wapakoneta, Ohio, USA.'

Neil Alden Armstrong was born on 5 August 1930,
on his grandparents' farm just outside the town of
Wapakoneta, Ohio. His parents' names were Stephen
and Viola Armstrong. Neil had a younger sister, June,
and a younger brother, Dean.

Stephen Armstrong worked as an accountant
for the state of Ohio. Because of his job, the
family often had to move from house to house.

Neil was interested in flying from a very early
age. When he was just two years old, his parents
took him to watch the aeroplanes taking off
and landing at Cleveland Municipal Airport.
He was so fascinated by the planes that he
did not want to leave.

Neil had to wait another four years for
his first aeroplane flight. One Sunday
morning, he was taken up by a pilot
who was visiting town to give plane
rides to local people.

What were you like at school?

'I always worked hard and wanted to do well.'

By the time Neil started school, he could already read well. At primary school, he was a very bright student. Neil enjoyed going to school and playing football with his friends. He also became a boy scout. But there was something he enjoyed even more – making model aeroplanes.

Neil made his first model plane when he was eight years old, and was soon hard at work on the next. At the age of ten, Neil got his first part-time job, mowing grass in the local cemetery, to earn enough money to pay for new and bigger planes. He later worked in a bakery, using his earnings to buy a baritone horn, which he played in the school band.

At high school in Wapakoneta, Neil worked hard, especially in science and maths. He was also a natural leader, and other students often came to him for help. Neil continued to play in the school band, and to work at various jobs. Juggling school and work was tiring, but Neil did not mind. After all, the money would pay for flying lessons!

How old were you when you started to fly?

'I was 16 years old when I qualified as a pilot.'

On 5 August 1946, Neil celebrated his sixteenth birthday by earning his pilot's licence. Flying was like a dream come true. But Neil was also fascinated by how planes worked. After high school, he went to Purdue University to study aeronautical engineering.

But a year and a half later, the Navy called him up to train as a fighter pilot in the Korean War. At just 20 years old, he was the youngest pilot in his squadron.

Neil's flying skills and bravery were tested to the full. Once, he was forced to bail out when his jet was hit by enemy fire.

In 1952, Neil returned to Purdue to continue his studies. Three years later he went to work as a research pilot, testing new aircraft. One of the newest planes he flew was the X-15 rocket plane. It flew faster and higher than any other aircraft – it was the closest thing yet to a spaceship.

How did you become an astronaut?

'I was picked by NASA for the *Gemini 8* mission.'

In the 1960s, the Americans began Project *Gemini*, a series of space flights. Neil applied to become an astronaut, and was accepted. His first flight in 1966 was aboard *Gemini 8*, which carried out the first successful link up with another rocket in space. At first things went smoothly. But then one of the thrusters failed and *Gemini 8* started to spin out of control. Neil managed to steady the spacecraft, but it had been a close thing.

Neil was praised for his quick thinking and piloting skills. And when NASA announced the crews for the *Apollo* flights, he was named commander of *Apollo 11* – the first mission to land on the Moon. The other crew members were Edwin 'Buzz' Aldrin and Michael Collins.

The astronauts began a tough programme of training. Apart from being very fit, they had to understand every detail of the mission. Most importantly, they had to know what to do in an emergency. Neil had no fears about the mission, but added, 'What I really want to be, in all honesty, is the first man back from the Moon.'

How did you get to the Moon?

'We travelled in a *Saturn V* space rocket.'

On 16 July 1969, Armstrong, Aldrin and Collins were woken early and had steak and eggs for breakfast. Then they put on their spacesuits and were driven to Cape Kennedy, Florida. Standing on the launch pad was the giant *Saturn V* rocket, which would blast them into space. The *Apollo 11* spacecraft was perched on top.

At 6.52 am, Armstrong entered *Apollo 11*, followed by Aldrin and Collins. Mission control started the countdown. 'Twelve, eleven, ten, nine…' *Saturn V*'s enormous engines began to fire. '… Six, five, four, three, two, one, zero, all engines running.' The ground shook and, with a deafening roar, *Saturn V* blasted into the air. It was 9.32 am. 'Lift off! We have a lift off … Lift off on *Apollo 11*.'

Within a few minutes of lift off, the rocket's first and second-stage engines had fired and fallen away. At 9.44 am, the third-stage engines fired, sending the spacecraft into orbit around the Earth. About two and a half hours later, they fired again, boosting the speed of *Apollo 11* to 39,000 kilometres per hour. The astronauts were on their way to the Moon!

When did you step on to the Moon?

'On 20 July 1969, at 10.56 am precisely.'

After three days travelling through space, *Apollo 11* went
into orbit around the Moon. Next day, Armstrong and Aldrin
put on their spacesuits and crawled into the lunar module,
Eagle. At 1.46 pm, *Eagle* began its descent to the Moon's
surface. All went well and *Eagle* made a perfect
landing near the Sea of Tranquility.
The first words sent back
to Earth were 'Houston.
Tranquility Base here.
The *Eagle* has landed.'

Armstrong and Aldrin ate
a meal, then put on their
helmets and gloves, and their
life-support system backpacks.
There is no air or water on the
Moon, and temperatures range from
freezing to 120°C. Each backpack had
an oxygen supply, temperature control
and a two-way radio. Without these,
the men would not survive. Finally,
they opened the hatch and Neil began
to climb down the ladder outside.

What did you do on the Moon?

'We collected samples of Moon rock.'

Neil was soon joined by Buzz Aldrin. Their spacesuits were bulky, but there was so little gravity they were able to move easily. And the surface was powdery but firm.

The two men set up a camera, and started work. They had only a few hours before their supplies ran out. They collected samples of Moon rock and dust, and set up a series of experiments. These would help scientists measure the distance between the Earth and the Moon more accurately, and build up a better picture of the Moon's surface. Armstrong and Aldrin also set up an American flag. Because there is no wind on the Moon, they had to stiffen it with wire. They even had a telephone call – from the President of the USA.

The astronauts returned to the *Eagle*, only to find that the switch that fired the engine had broken. If they couldn't fix it they would be trapped. But with some quick thinking they replaced it with a pen! The engine fired, and the top half of the module lifted off, leaving the bottom half on the Moon.

How long did you stay in space?

'We were up there for eight days.'

Three hours after leaving the Moon, *Eagle* reached the waiting command module, *Columbia*. Here the astronauts rejoined Michael Collins. The *Eagle* was sent into space, to crash on the Moon's surface, then they began their journey back to Earth. As they approached the Earth, the service module was also jettisoned.

On 24 July, eight days after leaving the Earth, *Columbia's* parachutes opened and it splashed down in the Pacific Ocean. Divers, wearing special protective suits, opened the hatch and the astronauts were taken by helicopter to a rescue ship. The first journey to the Moon had been a success.

Scientists were afraid that the astronauts might
have brought back some dangerous, unknown
'Moon-germs', which might cause disease
on Earth. So the three men had to spend the
next 18 days in quarantine inside a laboratory
in Houston. Here they spent much of their time
discussing their flight with people from NASA.

When the doctors were satisfied that the
astronauts were well and had no strange
germs, the astronauts were at last
allowed out to meet the world
and rejoin their families.

What happened when you got back to Earth?

'It was amazing. We were treated like heroes.'

The Moon mission had made Armstrong, Aldrin and Collins famous. Everyone wanted to see them or hear what they had to say about their experiences.

On 13 August, the three men and their wives visited three cities in the USA on a whirlwind one-day tour beginning in New York. Then it was on to Chicago and Los Angeles. They were also awarded the Presidential Medal of Freedom, the highest award for an American civilian.

NASA had organized a world tour for them. In 45 days, the astronauts visited 27 cities in 24 countries. At every stop on the route, thousands of people lined the streets to welcome them and cheer them on. When the tour ended, Neil took a job at NASA's headquarters in Washington DC. He also continued his studies in aerospace engineering.

But Neil Armstrong was a very private person, and did not always welcome the fame and attention. He did not like talking to newspaper interviewers and turned down most offers to advertise products. He wanted to live a private life as an ordinary person. Being the first man on the Moon made this almost impossible.

Did you ever go into space again?

'No, but I often wished
I was up there.'

In 1971, Neil resigned from NASA and taught aerospace engineering at the University of Cincinnati. He also studied how space technology could be used on Earth. In 1976, he headed a team developing a pump for use in open-heart surgery. It was based on a pump used in the *Apollo* spacesuits.

Neil never went into space again. He bought a farm in Ohio, and lived quietly with his family. He rarely appeared in public or gave interviews. In 1979, he resigned from his university post. Meanwhile the *Apollo* programme continued with six more Moon missions. But the next major step in space exploration came in the 1970s with the launch of the Russian and American space stations.

Neil was still interested in space exploration, and worked on a programme to take space exploration into the twenty-first century. The plan was never completed. On 28 January 1986, the space shuttle *Challenger* exploded seconds after lift-off. Neil was deputy chief of the committee set up to find out what caused the disaster.

In July 1994, people all over the USA celebrated the twenty-fifth anniversary of the first landing on the Moon. But Neil Armstrong did not take part in any of the official events. He did appear at a local airshow where, on seeing a plane fly overhead, he was heard to say, 'I wish I was up there.'

Saturn V

The gigantic *Saturn V* rocket
was the rocket that carried the
Apollo 11 astronauts into space.

Saturn V was built in
three stages, with the
Apollo 11 spacecraft
on top. The rocket
was 110.6 metres
tall and weighed
2.9 million kilograms.
It was the largest
rocket ever built.

After lift-off, the first-stage
engines fired for 2.5 minutes,
lifting the rocket to a height of
about 60 kilometres. Then the
first-stage rockets fell into the
Atlantic Ocean.

*first-stage
rocket*

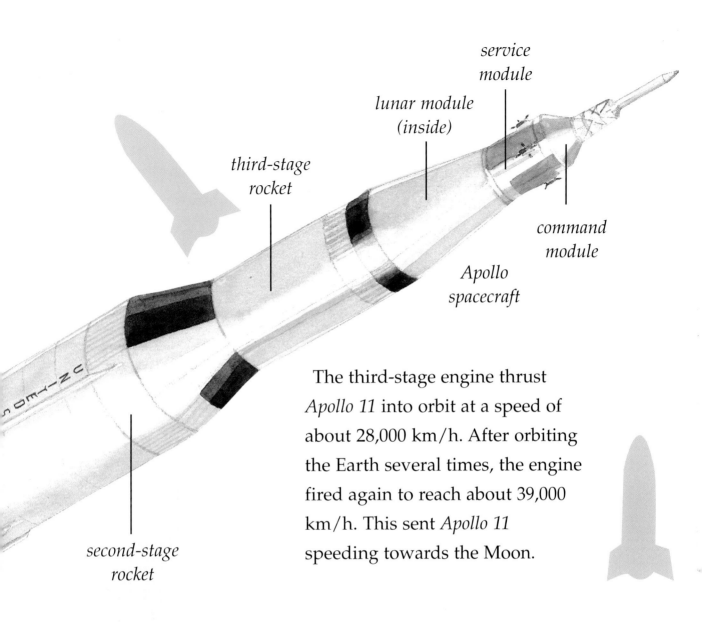

service
module

lunar module
(inside)

third-stage
rocket

command
module

Apollo
spacecraft

second-stage
rocket

The third-stage engine thrust *Apollo 11* into orbit at a speed of about 28,000 km/h. After orbiting the Earth several times, the engine fired again to reach about 39,000 km/h. This sent *Apollo 11* speeding towards the Moon.

The second-stage engines burned for about 6 minutes, taking the rocket to a height of about 185 kilometres at a speed of about 25,000 km/h. Then the second-stage engines fell away.

The only part of the *Apollo 11* aircraft to return to Earth was the command module with the three astronauts on board. It splashed down in the Pacific Ocean, supported by parachutes.

Some important dates

1930 Neil Armstrong is born on 5 August.

1936 Neil takes his first ride in an aeroplane. He is already fascinated by flying.

1946 On his sixteenth birthday, Neil gains his pilot's licence – before he passes his driving test.

1947 Neil finishes high school. He wins a Navy scholarship and goes to Purdue University to take a degree in aeronautical engineering.

1949 The Navy calls Neil up to train to fight in the Korean War.

1950–1953 The Korean War is fought in the Far East, between the USA and 19 other nations. Neil is sent to Korea as a fighter pilot and is awarded three air medals for outstanding service.

1952 Neil returns to the USA. He continues his studies at Purdue.

1955 Neil graduates from Purdue with a Bachelor of Science degree. He starts work as a research pilot.

1956 On 28 January, Neil marries Jan Sheardon.

1957 With the launch of the Russian *Sputnik 1* satellite, the 'space race' between the USSR and the USA begins.

1961 The Russian cosmonaut, Yuri Gagarin, becomes the first person in space.

1962 Neil is chosen to be an astronaut. He moves with his family to Houston, Texas. He spends his time training, and working on space projects.

1966 Neil is made commander of the *Gemini 8* space mission. The spacecraft makes the first successful link up with another rocket in space. This link up is called docking.

1969 *Apollo 11* is launched on 16 July. On 20 July, Neil is the first person on the Moon. He is followed by Buzz Aldrin.

1971 Neil leaves NASA and becomes a professor at Cincinnati University. He buys a farm near Lebanon, Ohio.

1978 Neil receives the Congressional Space Medal of Honor.

1979–1982 Neil leaves Cincinnati University. He serves on the board of various companies.

1984 Neil works for the National Commission on Space (NCOS).

1986 The space shuttle *Challenger* explodes seconds after lift-off, killing all seven astronauts on board. Neil is part of the team finding out what happened.

1994 Celebrations are held all across the USA to mark the twenty-fifth anniversary of the Moon landing, but Neil does not take part.

1998 American astronaut John Glenn goes into space on board the shuttle. At 77, he is the oldest person in space. His mission is to test the effect of space on growing old.

Glossary

aeronautical engineering
Building aircraft and improving aircraft design.

aerospace engineering
Building rockets and spacecraft and improving their design.

Apollo The name given to the spacecraft that took people to the Moon. *Apollo* spacecraft were blasted into space by huge rockets. The spacecraft itself was made up of three parts, the **command module**, the **lunar module** and the **service module**.

astronaut Someone who travels in space.

bail out To jump out of a flying aircraft in an emergency, using a parachute.

baritone horn A low-sounding musical instrument.

civilian Someone who is not in the armed forces.

command module
The cone-shaped part of the *Apollo* spacecraft that the astronauts lived in, and used to return to Earth.

cosmonaut The name for a Russian astronaut.

docking One spacecraft or rocket joining up with another in space.

fighter pilot Someone who flies an aeroplane that is designed to fire at other aircraft.

gravity A natural force that pulls objects towards each other.

jettison To throw away, cast off.

launch pad A platform from which a spacecraft is blasted into space by the power of a rocket.

life-support system Equipment that keeps a person alive.

lunar module The part of the *Apollo* spacecraft that landed on the Moon.

Mission A special task.

NASA The National Aeronautics and Space Administration. It is the organization that works on space projects in the United States.

orbit The path one object takes around another in space.

quarantine To be kept apart from all other people and animals.

research pilot Someone who tests aircraft by flying them.

rocket A flying machine driven by burning gases that powers aircraft and spacecraft.

satellite A man-made satellite is an object that is launched into space from Earth. It orbits the Earth, Moon or another planet, and sends information back to Earth.

service module The part of the *Apollo* spacecraft that carried the rocket engine, fuel and oxygen.

space shuttle A spacecraft that returns to Earth after each mission and can be used again.

space station A large spacecraft that stays in orbit round Earth for a long time. Astronauts can live and work there, collecting scientific information, and other spacecraft can visit it.

thruster A small rocket that is used to push a spacecraft to the correct height and in the correct direction.

Index